Old Babylonia

Children's Middle Eastern History Books

Speedy Publishing LLC
40 E. Main St. #1156
Newark, DE 19711
www.speedypublishing.com

Copyright 2016

All Rights reserved. No part of this book may be reproduced or used in any way or form or by any means whether electronic or mechanical, this means that you cannot record or photocopy any material ideas or tips that are provided in this book

Hi, kids! Let's learn about ancient Babylon. Turn the pages and marvel at this fantastic city from the past – the fabulous city of Babylon!

Over 3000 years ago, Babylonia became a city-state in Mesopotamia and the center of Mesopotamian civilization. Babylon was its capital. It was in southern Mesopotamia between the Tigris and Euphrates rivers.

Babylon was near the Persian Gulf. The Babylonians thought of it as "The Gate of the Gods". It was believed that the City of Babylon was built to honor the most powerful god of all Babylonians, Marduk.

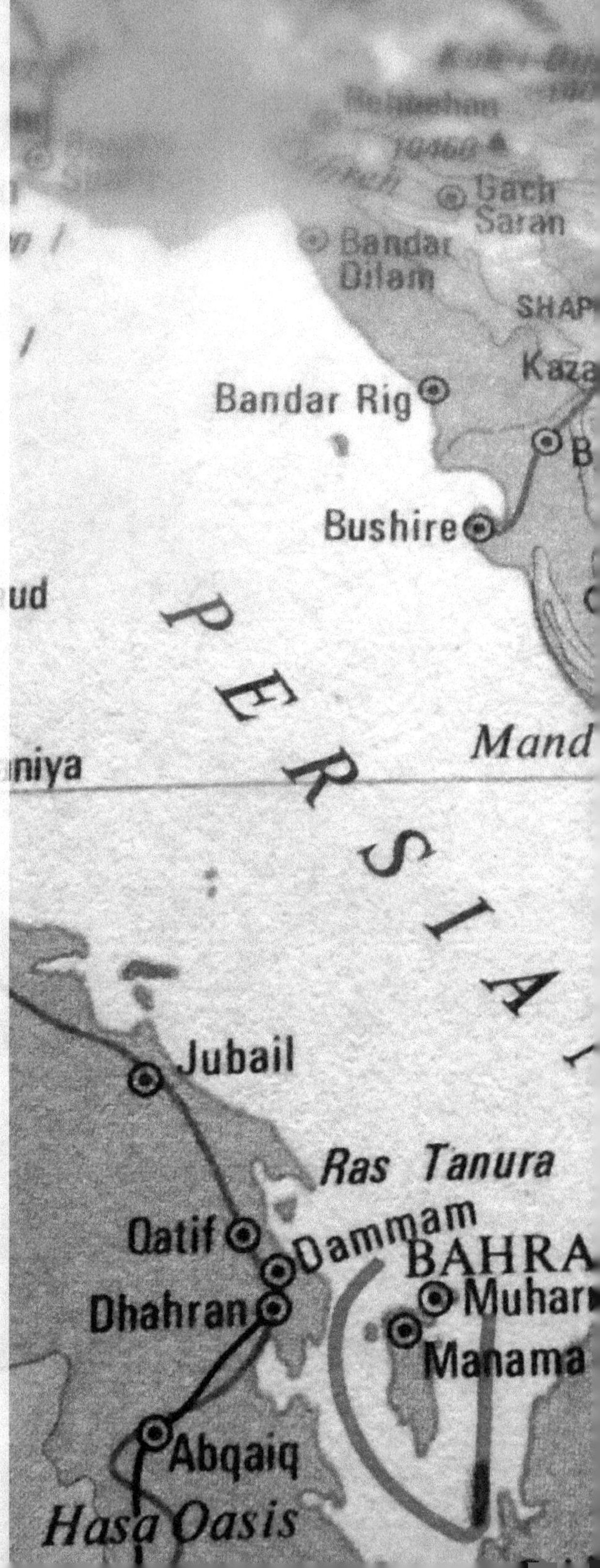

OUNTAINS

Pulvar

Deh Bid

Kuh-i-Masahim
11350

Kur

Tasak

PERSEPOLIS

Shiraz

Niriz

Fasa

Istehbanat

Firuzabad

Jahrom

Furg

Shur

Daulatabad

ngan

Lar

Gilehdar

Bastak

Ishqanan

Bandar Abbas

Qishm

Qishm I.

Str. of Hormuz

Bandar-e-Lengeh

GULF

8200

(Oman)

Khor

Umm-al-Gawein

Sharjah

Inspired by the Sumerians, the Babylonians used the cuneiform system, a written language, to keep records and send messages.

The two rising empires of Mesopotamia were the Babylonians in the south and the Assyrians to the north. The first empire to conquer all of Mesopotamia was the Babylonian Empire.

Hammurabi was a Babylonian king who created the earliest known set of written laws, known as the Code of Hammurabi.

The laws were recorded on clay tablets and on tall stone pillars called steles.

As king, Hammurabi fought wars and turned Babylonia into an empire after the fall of the Akkadian Empire. The discipline of a soldier shows in his Code, for the Babylonian laws were severe.

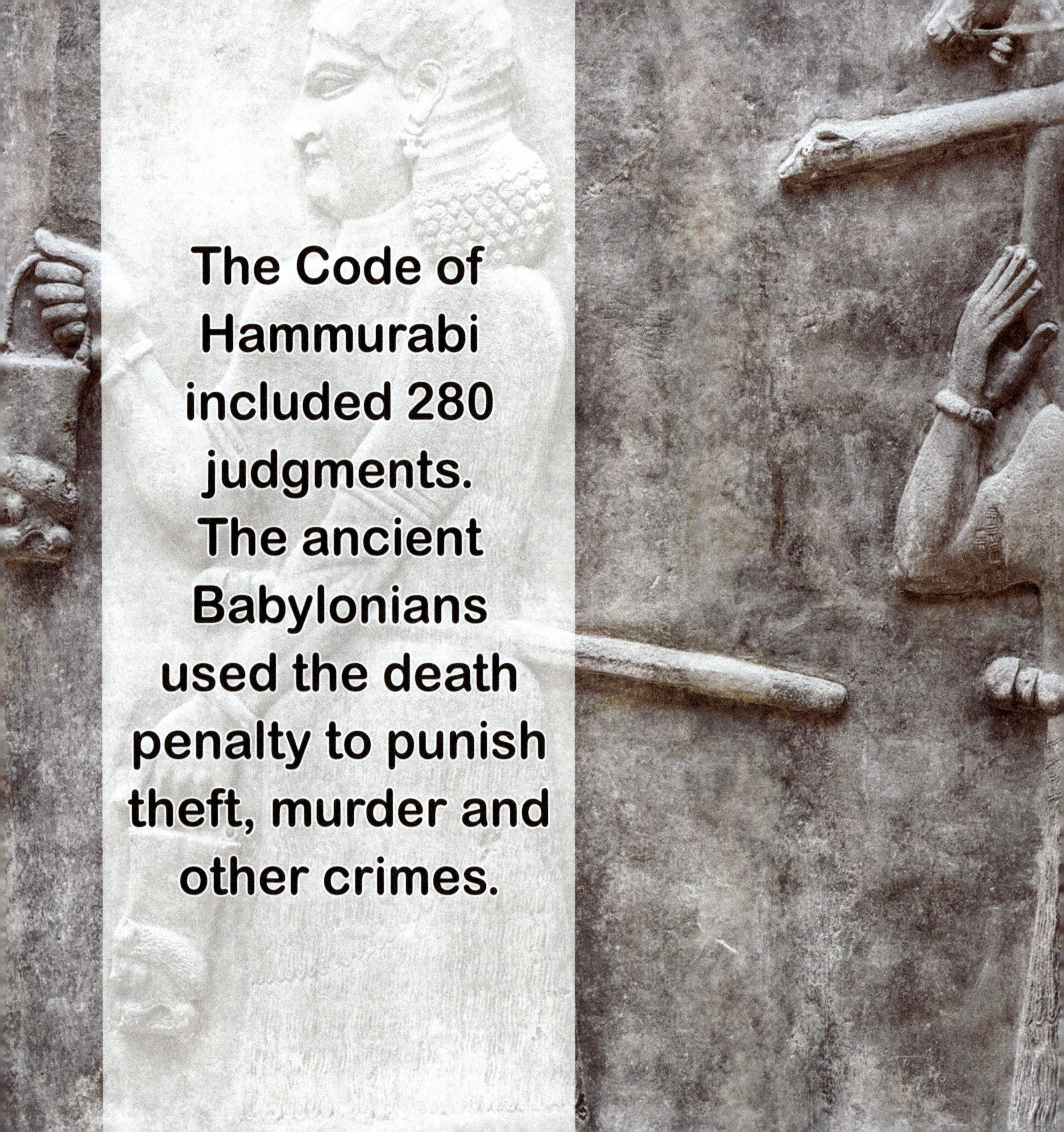
The Code of Hammurabi included 280 judgments. The ancient Babylonians used the death penalty to punish theft, murder and other crimes.

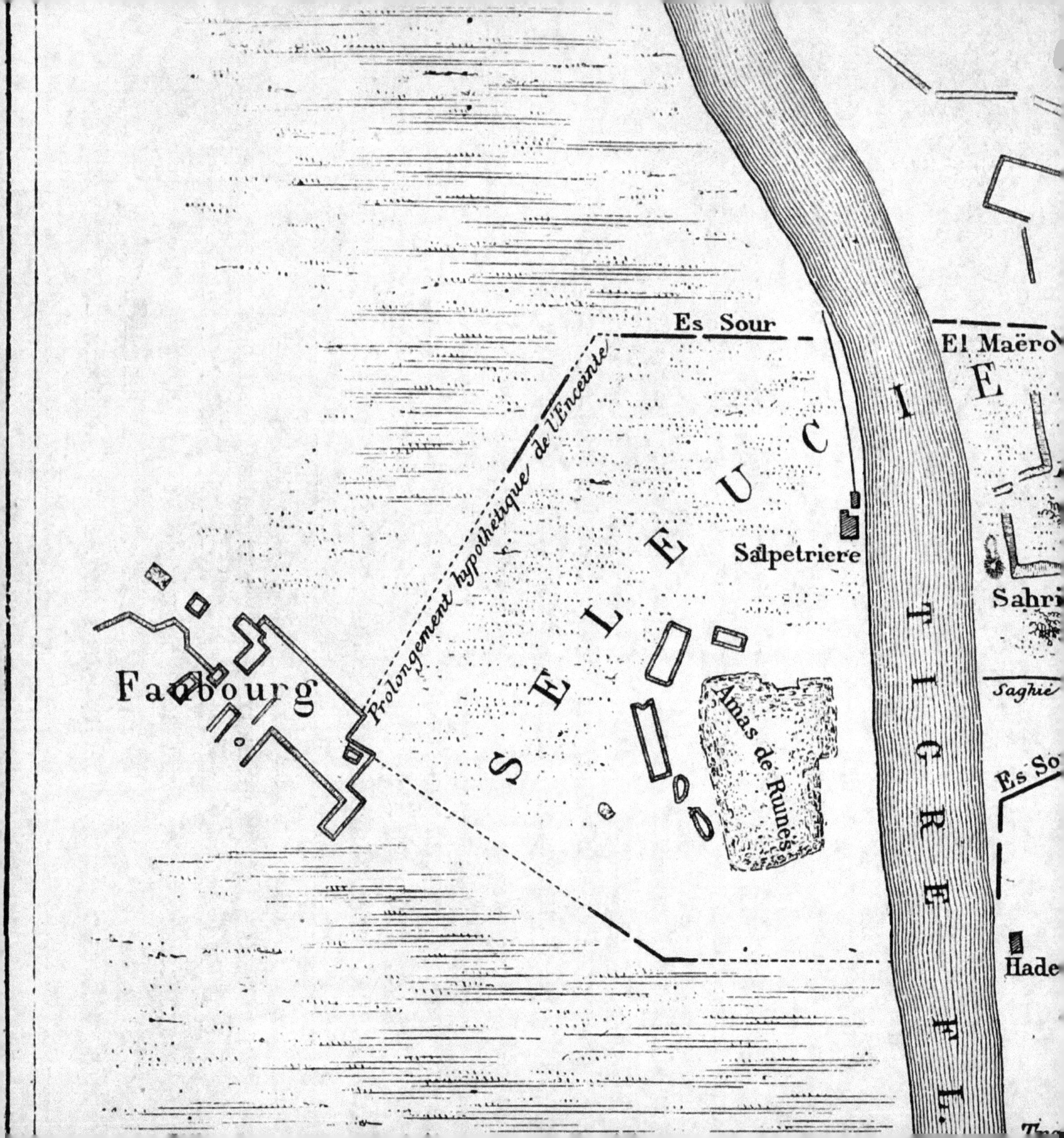

Es Sour

El Maëro

SELEUCIE

Prolongement hypothétique de l'Enceinte

Salpetriere

Sahri

Saghie

Faubourg

Amas de Ruines

Es So

Hade

TIGRE FL.

The Rise of Ancient Babylonia

PLAN
de
SELEUCIE - CTÉSIPHON
levé en Avril 1866
G. LEJEAN

Echelle

0 500 1000 1500 pas

ell Zembil

Hod

Ziaret de Salman Pak

Tak Kesra

Kaber Chaha

Ed D'bai

Tell Arak

mani

Es Sour

Tell el Bagh

Babylonia began to rise in 1792 BC when the Sumerian civilization lost power. King Hammurabi came to power and ruled land far beyond the city of Babylon.

In fact, he was able to conquer the city states in Mesopotamia which included much of the Assyrian lands of the north.

Under the rule of King Hammurabi, Babylonia became the most powerful city in the world. The city's growth was partly due to its location.

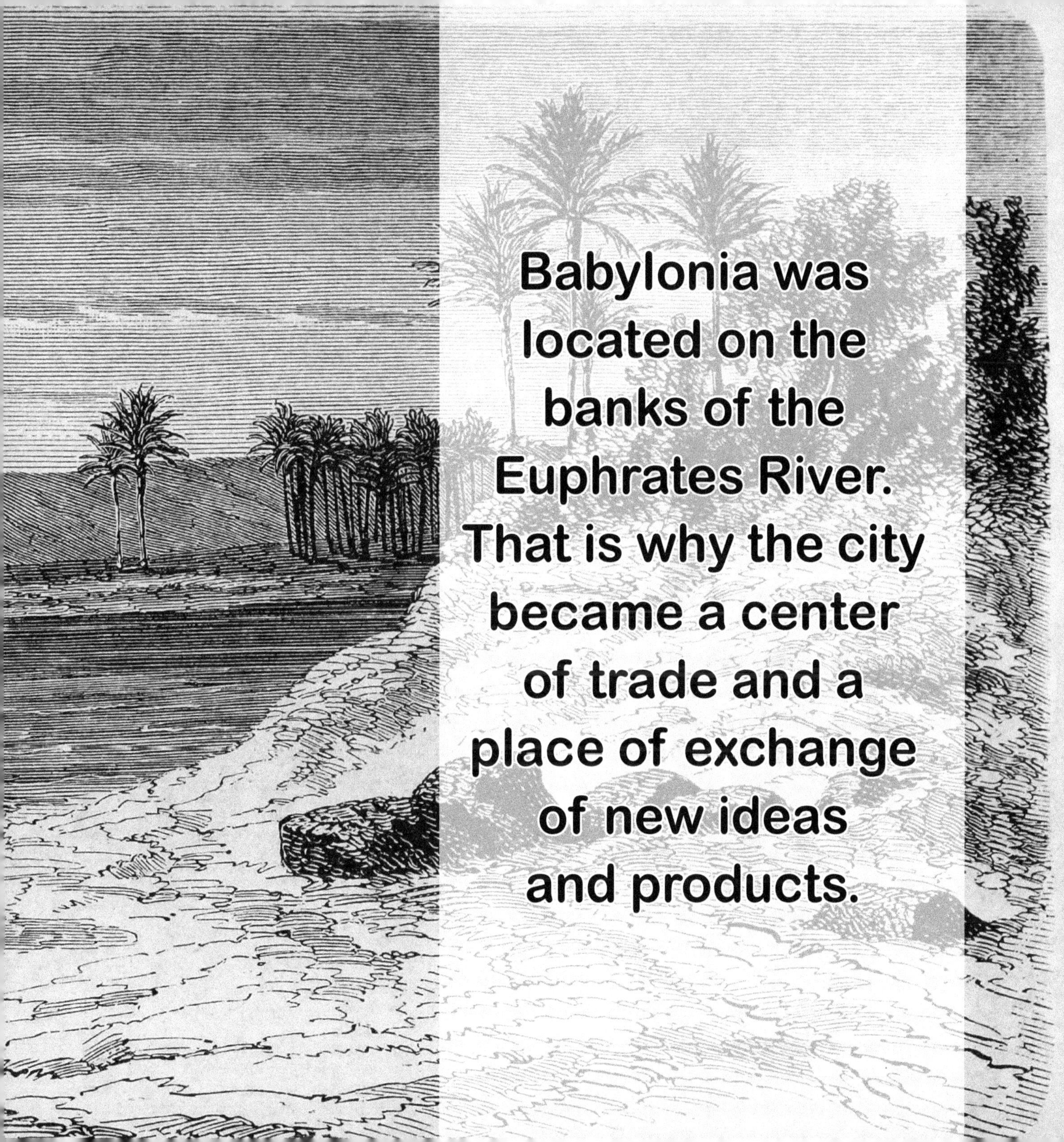
Babylonia was
located on the
banks of the
Euphrates River.
That is why the city
became a center
of trade and a
place of exchange
of new ideas
and products.

During this time, Babylonia had a population of 200,000 people. Babylon was at that time the largest city in the world.

The Ziggurat was a large temple, approximately 300 ft in height built at the center of the Babylon. The temple looked like a pyramid with flat top.

Babylonia became famous because of its artwork. The amazing gardens, palaces and towers were the pride of the city. Being the cultural center of the empire, Babylon had a great display of art, science, music, astronomy, literature, mathematics and other disciplines.

One of the greatest accomplishments of the Mesopotamian civilization was the construction of the Hanging Gardens of Babylon. It became one of the wonders of the ancient world. It is believed that the hanging gardens were built by Nebuchadnezzar II, a king mentioned in the Bible.

Even the ruins of the city demonstrate that ancient Babylon was once a precious jewel in Mesopotamia!

Visit

BABY PROFESSOR
EDUCATION KIDS

www.BabyProfessorBooks.com

to download Free Baby Professor eBooks and view our catalog of new and exciting Children's Books

www.ingramcontent.com/pod-product-compliance
Lightning Source LLC
LaVergne TN
LVHW060831170826
845678LV00010B/1956
9798869442901